HAPPY Birthday Grandpa

The Life Graduate Publishing Group

No part of this book may be scanned, reproduced or distributed in any printed or electronic form without the prior permission of the author or publisher.
Copyright - The Life Graduate Publishing Group 2020 - All Rights Reserved

★★★★★

We love to receive reviews from our customers. If you had the opportunity to provide a review we would greatly appreciate it.
Thank you!

Birthday

I Wrote This Book For You Grandpa!

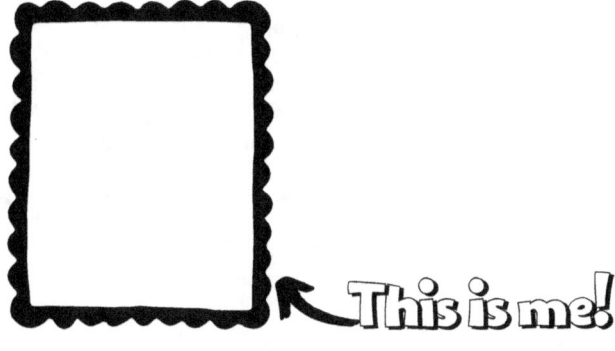
This is me!

Created By: _____

Birthday Year: _____

My Age: _____ yrs

We celebrate your birthday on..

MONTH _____

DAY _____

I love birthday cake!!

Happy Birthday Grandpa. I wrote this book for you because......

_____

_____

_____

_____

_____

This is a drawing of us together on your birthday.

Grandpa and I

4

I LOVE YOU BECAUSE...

Grandpa, my favorite place to visit with you is....

These are 3 things you do that are kind.

My favorite birthday food is...

Place your hand here and trace around it with a pencil

You like to relax by doing this..

_____

_____

_____

My favorite photo!

I would like you to teach me how to do this...

If I could get you anything in the whole wide-world for your birthday it would be...

13

You make me laugh when..

If I created a birthday t-shirt for you, it would look like this...

Create your special design here!

It might look like this or something different?

You can do this better than anyone else!

This is a drawing of us on your birthday.

I hope that one day we can do this together..

You cook the best......

19

I colored in this birthday cake for you!

These are 3 words that best describe you.

1. _____

2. _____

3. _____

SPECIAL MOMENTS or MEMORIES

Add other special photo's or drawings here ↙

SPECIAL MOMENTS or MEMORIES

Add other special photo's or drawings here

SPECIAL MOMENTS or MEMORIES

Add other special photo's or drawings here

SPECIAL MOMENTS or MEMORIES

Add other special photo's or drawings here

Color me in!

THIS HAS BEEN MY SPECIAL BIRTHDAY GIFT THAT I HAVE CREATED FOR YOU.

I HOPE YOU LIKE IT!

A sample of other books created by Romney Nelson

THE LIFE GRADUATE PUBLISHING GROUP

www.thelifegraduate.com/bookstore

www.ingramcontent.com/pod-product-compliance
Lightning Source LLC
LaVergne TN
LVHW060144080526
838202LV00049B/4083